T0054099

Who Was
Charles Dickens?

Who Was
Charles Dickens?

by Pam Pollack and Meg Belviso

illustrated by Mark Edward Geyer

Penguin Workshop

To Paula Manzanero and the ghosts of books
past, present, and future—PP & MB

For my mother, Joan Lavigueur Geyer, a great artist. What you
taught me cannot be measured—MEG

PENGUIN WORKSHOP
An Imprint of Penguin Random House LLC, New York

Text copyright © 2014 by Pam Pollack and Meg Belviso.
Illustrations copyright © 2014 by Penguin Random House LLC. All rights reserved.
Published by Penguin Workshop, an imprint of Penguin Random House LLC, New York.
PENGUIN and PENGUIN WORKSHOP are trademarks of Penguin Books Ltd.
WHO HQ & Design is a registered trademark of Penguin Random House LLC.
Printed in the USA.

Visit us online at www.penguinrandomhouse.com.

Library of Congress Control Number: 2014958190

ISBN 9780448479675   10 9 8 7

Contents

Who Was Charles Dickens?....................................1

Welcome to London....................................5

Hidden Talents....................................19

Introducing Boz....................................28

A Whole New World....................................38

Scrooges and Micawbers....................................49

Back to Gad's Hill....................................61

The Worst of Times....................................70

New Journeys....................................75

Terror to the End....................................83

Poet's Corner....................................93

Timelines....................................102

Bibliography....................................104

Who Was
Charles Dickens?

On Chandos Street in London, just northwest of Covent Garden's bustling markets, Warren's factory produced blacking paste, which was used for shoe polish. In 1824, there was a curious show in the window of Warren's blacking factory.

Ladies and gentleman were often drawn to the window to see it.

Two boys, one twelve years old, the other a little older, sat side by side. Their job was to seal and label the blacking jars. They worked six days a week for ten hours a day. The boys had to be quick to get their work done. To make the day interesting they'd made a game of it, competing to see who could be fastest.

They were so speedy that people on the street stopped to stare at them.

The older boy was an orphan named Bob Fagin. He didn't mind people watching him work. The other boy was Charles Dickens. For him, sitting in the window of Warren's blacking factory was the worst thing he could imagine.

Charles dreamed of going to school, maybe even one of the great English universities like Oxford or Cambridge. He loved to read and sometimes even wrote stories of his own. John Dickens, Charles's father, always spent more money than he earned. When John fell into debt, he could no longer afford his family of seven children. So Charles was taken out of school and sent to work. He was heartbroken and embarrassed. What if he spent his whole life trapped in a factory window, laughed at by people on the street? He couldn't believe his parents had done this to him. He prayed to be "lifted out of the humiliation and neglect."

When Charles grew up, he would write many stories about poor children living lonely, harsh lives. His stories would become some of the most widely read and beloved books in the world.

It wasn't until after his death that people learned Charles Dickens was once one of those poor children, too.

Chapter 1
Welcome to London

Charles Dickens was born in Portsmouth, England, on February 7, 1812. His father, John, worked for the Navy Pay Office. John earned a steady salary and he liked to spend money on himself, his friends, his wife, and his two children, Fanny and Charles. Over the next few years, the Dickenses would have seven children in all. With so many children, and a limited salary, John needed to be very careful about how he spent his money. Unfortunately, John was never careful about money. If he didn't have money to pay for bread, he would put it on a bill at the baker's to

pay later. By the time the baker was demanding to be paid, John owed money to many other people—the shoemaker, the butcher, the tailor. Even then, instead of saving every penny to pay them back, he would have an expensive meal at a restaurant. He always just imagined he'd find the money somewhere, but he never did.

When Charles was five, his family moved
to Chatham, a naval town on the Thames
River. Charles loved Chatham. He had lots of

other children to play with. He enjoyed school. Sometimes Charles did not feel well. He suffered with pains in his side that kept him in bed. But his family had a nursemaid—a young woman who looked after the children. She was named Mary Weller. Mary told wonderful—and terrifying—bedtime stories to Charles.

He also loved to read on his own. His favorite books were *Peregrine Pickle*, *Tom Jones,* and *Tales of*

the Arabian Nights. Sometimes he wrote stories of his own, like "Misnar, Sultan of India." He hoped one day to become as good a storyteller as Mary.

Sometimes Charles and his father took walks around the town. One day they stopped in front of a beautiful house on Gad's Hill. It was large and made of brick with a view of the whole countryside. Charles said he would like to live in that house one day. His father told him that if he worked very hard, one day he might do so.

In 1822, when Charles was ten, his father was transferred to London, the capital city of England. The Dickens family moved to a neighborhood called Camden Town. London was a new world for Charles. There were over 1.3 million people living in London at that time. That was two hundred thousand more people than just twenty years earlier. London was growing fast.

New inventions had led to an increase in factory work. People who once lived in the country now moved to the city for factory jobs. These jobs were often low-paying, and there were not enough of them for all the people coming to London.

Many children had to take care of themselves while their parents worked. The streets were dirty and noisy. They were filled with people, as well as carts, horses, and pigs. Hungry, barefoot children dressed in rags played in the streets and begged for money. School was a luxury only families with money could afford.

At the Dickenses' home in Camden Town, Charles slept in a cupboard —like a closet—over the main stairway. Charles's older sister, Fanny, was sent to the Royal Academy of Music to study singing.

Charles no longer went to school at all. There wasn't enough money.

Charles's mother had plans to start a school of her own. She sent him out to advertise the new school, but the only people who came were people to whom his father owed money. They banged on the door while his father hid upstairs. Sometimes John Dickens sent Charles to the pawnshop on Hampstead Road. Charles was sent out with dishes, furniture, and even his beloved books.

The family lived huddled in two empty rooms with no money to pay for coal for the fire. They had sold everything they owned to the pawnshop.

Even in this difficult time, Charles was growing to love London. He liked to listen to people talk on the street. He learned their accents and gestures and the slang they used. Whenever he heard an interesting story about someone, he remembered it.

Then a friend of the family had an idea. Charles could earn money working at Warren's blacking factory. For Charles this was terrible news. He felt as if his parents didn't think his life was worth anything.

At the blacking factory—at 30 Strand and then later on Chandos Street—Charles worked with two other boys, Bob Fagin and Poll Green. Charles was supposed to have lessons during his short dinner break. But the lessons didn't last long. He lived like every other factory boy, working ten hours a day, six days a week.

Bob and Poll sometimes called
Charles the "young gentleman" because he
spoke and behaved like someone who had been
educated. In England at that time, it would have
been very unusual for a poor boy like Bob Fagin
to ever advance into "polite" or high society.
Charles was afraid that he would become a factory
worker for life, just as Bob probably would be.

CHILD LABOR

THE GROWTH OF FACTORIES AND BUSINESSES IN THE NINETEENTH CENTURY MEANT MANY CHILDREN WERE SENT TO WORK. CHILDREN AS YOUNG AS FOUR YEARS OLD HAD JOBS. THEY WORKED UP TO SIXTEEN HOURS A DAY IN DANGEROUS CONDITIONS. SOMETIMES THEY WERE BEATEN IF THEY DIDN'T WORK HARD ENOUGH. POOR FAMILIES DEPENDED ON THE MONEY THEIR CHILDREN EARNED AS TRADE APPRENTICES, MACHINE OPERATORS, HOUSEHOLD SERVANTS, AND COAL MINERS. YOUNG CHILDREN WORKED AT FACTORIES MAKING EVERYTHING FROM BLANKETS TO MATCHES TO NAILS. THE PAY WAS AS LITTLE AS A HALF A PENNY PER HOUR. BY THE EARLY DECADES OF THE TWENTIETH CENTURY, PEOPLE WERE BECOMING OUTRAGED BY THE CRUELTIES OF CHILD LABOR. CURRENTLY, ALMOST EVERY COUNTRY IN THE WORLD HAS LAWS AIMED AT PREVENTING CHILD LABOR.

Charles's small salary wasn't enough to pay his father's debts. On February 20, 1824, John Dickens was thrown into the Marshalsea Prison because of all the money he owed.

Chapter 2
Hidden Talents

The Marshalsea Prison was a debtors' prison. John Dickens had to stay there until he paid what he owed.

Except for Charles and Fanny, the whole family moved into Marshalsea Prison. Fanny boarded at her music school, and Charles moved in with Mrs. Roylance, a woman who rented rooms to working children. She didn't treat Charles very well.

MARSHALSEA PRISON

MARSHALSEA PRISON IN SOUTHWARK, LONDON, WAS FOUNDED IN THE 1300S ON THE BANK OF THE RIVER THAMES. IT HELD PEOPLE WHO HAD COMMITTED MANY DIFFERENT CRIMES, INCLUDING ACCUMULATING LARGE DEBTS. SOMETIMES ENTIRE FAMILIES WERE IMPRISONED, NOT JUST THE PARENT WHO HAD COMMITTED A CRIME. IF THE PRISONERS HAD SOME MONEY, THEY COULD BUY THINGS AT THE PRISON SHOPS OR RESTAURANTS AND LIVE IN ONE OF THE NICER ROOMS. THEY

COULD ALSO BUY A PASS TO LEAVE THE PRISON AND EARN THE MONEY TO PAY OFF THEIR DEBTS. MANY PRISONERS RACKED UP MORE DEBTS WHILE IN PRISON, AND THE POOREST PEOPLE WERE CRAMMED INTO THE WORST ROOMS. MANY STARVED TO DEATH WITHIN MONTHS.

MARSHALSEA PRISON WAS TORN DOWN IN THE 1870S. ONLY A SINGLE WALL REMAINS, WHERE A PLAQUE WITH A QUOTE FROM CHARLES DICKENS READS: "IT IS GONE NOW, AND THE WORLD IS NONE THE WORSE WITHOUT IT."

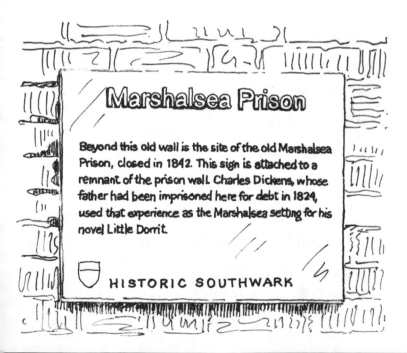

Marshalsea Prison

Beyond this old wall is the site of the old Marshalsea Prison, closed in 1842. This sign is attached to a remnant of the prison wall. Charles Dickens, whose father had been imprisoned here for debt in 1824, used that experience as the Marshalsea setting for his novel Little Dorrit.

HISTORIC SOUTHWARK

Every Sunday, Charles and Fanny would walk twelve miles to visit the family. On one of these visits, Charles convinced his father to find him a nicer place to stay, but he never forgot the terrible Mrs. Roylance.

His father's troubles had made Charles terrified of debt. When he got his own pay each week, he divided the coins into seven equal piles. He wrapped those in little sacks and wrote the name of each day of the week on a different stack of coins. The sack for Wednesday would never be opened until that day. In this way, Charles learned to spend money only when necessary.

In May 1824, John Dickens was released from prison. He had inherited enough money to pay off his debts. Soon Charles no longer had to work at Warren's.

His mother was angry that Charles was no longer working. She wanted to send him back. To Charles, his father was a hero for rescuing him from the factory, and his mother was a villain. "I never afterwards forgot, I never shall forget, I never can forget, that my mother was warm for my being sent back," Charles said. The family never spoke of it again.

Charles returned to school. At Wellington House Academy, the teachers were strict,

but Charles loved it. After so many months at the
factory, he threw himself into games, theater,
and jokes. He hid mice and bees in his desk, and
made tiny stagecoaches for the mice to ride.

He wrote stories and started his own newspaper.
Other boys paid for copies with marbles. He made
the boys laugh by pretending to speak in a foreign
language he had made up himself.

Only two years later, when Charles was fifteen,
his father fell into debt once again and could no
longer pay for school. Charles went to work as a clerk
at the Ellis and Blackmore law firm in May 1827.

On his first day, he wore a military-style cap that
tied under his chin. When his new bosses sent

him out on an errand, he came back with a black eye!

Charles explained that a man in the street had made fun of his cap and knocked it off, and they had gotten into a fight. His bosses weren't shocked by the story, but they were shocked by how he told the story. He acted it out for them, playing both parts, plus the parts of onlookers.

When he imitated the man making fun of his hat, his bosses couldn't stop laughing.

The more they spoke to their young clerk, the more amazed Ellis and Blackmore were by how well he knew London—the streets, the stories, the colorful characters. Their new clerk had hidden talents as a storyteller!

Chapter 3
Introducing Boz

Charles worked as a law clerk until 1829.
When he was seventeen, he became a newspaper
reporter in the law courts. Sometimes he wrote
funny stories that pointed out the unfairness of

the laws at that time. For Charles, the courts were another place to observe how people behaved and to hear interesting stories.

At this same time, Charles met a young woman named Maria Beadnell. She was the daughter of a banker. Charles fell madly in love with her. Some nights after leaving the court at two in the morning, he walked miles to stand in front of her house. He wrote letters to her parents.

He said what a good match he was for their daughter, even though he didn't have much money.

Maria's family was not impressed. Her mother never even bothered to get Charles's name right. She referred to him as "Mr. Dickin." In 1832, Maria's parents sent her away to Paris.

With Maria gone, Charles focused on his writing. By the end of 1833, Charles had written a funny story about two cousins having dinner. He dropped the story, called "Dinner at Poplar Walk" into a "dark letter-box, in a dark office, up a dark court in Fleet Street." This was the office of the *Monthly Magazine.* A few days later, Charles bought a copy of the magazine and found the story printed there!

Charles's name didn't appear with the story. He didn't even get paid for it, but *Monthly Magazine* wanted more stories from the young writer. Instead of signing himself "Charles Dickens" in the magazine, he used the name "Boz." He borrowed the name from his youngest brother, Augustus, who was nicknamed Moses. As a toddler, Augustus pronounced it as "Boses," which became "Boz" for short.

Charles wanted to write a longer story about a group of friends who form a club. *The Pickwick Papers*, his first novel, wasn't published as a book at first. Instead, it appeared one chapter a month, starting in March 1836. People loved Charles's characters, especially the servant Sam Weller.

Samuel Weller

Charles wrote Weller's words with a Cockney accent, the very way he had heard people speak on the streets of London: "Werry sorry to 'casion any personal inconvenience, ma'am, as the house-breaker said to the old lady when he put her on the fire . . ."

Everyone was talking about *The Pickwick Papers* and Boz. No one knew that Charles Dickens was the real author of the novel. But that would soon change.

SERIALIZED BOOKS

IN THE NINETEENTH CENTURY, MANY BOOKS
WERE WRITTEN ONE CHAPTER AT A TIME. A SINGLE
CHAPTER WOULD BE PUBLISHED IN A MAGAZINE
EACH MONTH. A MAGAZINE WAS USUALLY THIRTY-
TWO PAGES AND CAME WRAPPED IN GREEN PAPER.
PEOPLE WOULD BUY EACH ISSUE OF THE MAGAZINE
TO READ THE NEXT PART OF THE STORY. THIS
WAS GOOD FOR PUBLISHERS, BECAUSE IT MADE
PEOPLE EAGER TO BUY MAGAZINES. FOR PEOPLE
WHO DIDN'T HAVE MUCH MONEY, A FEW PENNIES A
MONTH WAS AN AFFORDABLE WAY TO READ A NOVEL.

ONCE THE WHOLE STORY WAS COMPLETE,

THE PUBLISHER WOULD SELL A BOUND BOOK.
THOSE WHO COULD AFFORD IT BOUGHT THE STORY
AS A BOOK.

CHARLES DICKENS HAD CONTRACTS WITH MORE
THAN ONE PUBLISHER. EACH CONTRACT WAS
AN AGREEMENT THAT CHARLES WOULD WRITE A
BOOK IN INSTALLMENTS FOR THAT PUBLISHER.
HIS FIRST NOVEL, *THE PICKWICK PAPERS*, WAS
PUBLISHED BY CHAPMAN AND HALL. *OLIVER
TWIST*, WHICH HE WROTE AT THE SAME TIME,
WAS PUBLISHED IN THE MAGAZINE *BENTLEY'S
MISCELLANY* AND PUBLISHED BY RICHARD BENTLEY.

Now that Charles was becoming successful, he felt it was time to get married. There wasn't anyone he loved the way he had Maria Beadnell, but in the winter of 1836 he had met Catherine Hogarth through her father, a newspaper editor.

CATHERINE HOGARTH

If Charles wasn't exactly in love with Catherine, he did *like* her an awful lot, and he was very good friends with her younger sister, Mary. On April 2, 1836, Catherine and Charles were married. A month later they were expecting their first child.

Chapter 4
A Whole New World

Charles and Catherine moved to the Holborn neighborhood of London with Catherine's sister Mary.

Even though he hadn't yet finished *The Pickwick Papers*, Charles signed a contract to start a new novel. *Oliver Twist* is the story of an orphan boy who is kicked out of a workhouse for asking for more food. He runs away to London and falls in with a gang of thieves. The gang's leaders are the Artful Dodger and the villainous Fagin,

Oliver Twist begs for food.

who was named after Charles's old friend at the blacking factory.

Charles wrote both novels at once, scribbling madly with his quill pen. Every month he wrote one chapter for each book. The two books were very different. When the hero of *The Pickwick Papers* was having funny adventures, Oliver Twist was running for his life.

In addition to writing for *Monthly Magazine*, Charles quit court reporting and became the editor of a newspaper, *Bentley's Miscellany*.

THE WORKHOUSE

A WORKHOUSE WAS A PLACE WHERE THE POOR IN ENGLAND COULD WORK IN EXCHANGE FOR THEIR FOOD AND HOUSING. BECAUSE MANY OF THE WORKHOUSE RESIDENTS HAD NO SKILLS, THEY OFTEN HAD TO DO DIFFICULT, BUT BORING, WORK LIKE BREAKING STONES AND UNRAVELING OLD ROPES SO THAT THE FIBERS COULD BE REUSED. LIFE IN A WORKHOUSE WAS NOT PLEASANT,

BUT IT WAS BETTER THAN LIVING ON THE STREET. CHILDREN IN WORKHOUSES RECEIVED SOME EDUCATION AND MEDICAL CARE, WHICH THEY WOULDN'T HAVE GOTTEN OUTSIDE THE WORKHOUSE. IT WAS NOT UNTIL THE PASSING OF THE NATIONAL ASSISTANCE ACT OF 1948 THAT THE LAST WORKHOUSE IN ENGLAND WAS CLOSED.

He chose stories, made sure they were printed correctly, and helped other writers. Most people would consider any *one* of these jobs—writing a novel, writing a second novel, or editing *Bentley's*—to be full-time work. Charles did all three at once and was also writing a play at the same time!

Charles's son, Charley, was born in January 1837. Charles called his new son "the infant phenomenon." He wrote the scene of Oliver Twist's birth just a few weeks after Charley was born and probably used his own son for inspiration.

Life at home was happy. Then, on May 7, 1837, Charles heard a scream from his sister-in-law Mary's room. She was very sick. She had been perfectly well just minutes before, and she was only seventeen. Yet the next afternoon, Mary died in Charles's arms. Doctors thought it might have been her heart.

That month there were no new chapters of *The Pickwick Papers* or *Oliver Twist*. Charles was too heartbroken to write. It was the only time in his career he ever missed a deadline.

After Mary's death, Charles and Catherine took a vacation away from London. Charles spent a lot of time with a new friend, John Forster, a literary editor. It was a friendship that would last the rest of his life.

JOHN FORSTER

Charles's next books, including *Nicholas Nickleby* and *Barnaby Rudge*, were all published under his real name. His book *The Old Curiosity Shop* became so popular in America that when ships arrived with the magazines that contained a new chapter, people shouted from the docks for news about its young heroine: "Does Little Nell still live?" Charles thought a lot about visiting America. He often received fan mail from his American readers.

On January 2, 1842, Charles and Catherine traveled by steamship to the United States. They left their children—Charley and two daughters, Mamie and Katey—behind in England.

There were many things Charles didn't like about America. American publishers had been making money off his books without paying him! When Charles complained, reporters published stories about him that were not very kind. Crowds of American fans followed him everywhere. Newspapers said that Charles had "more animation than grace and more intelligence than beauty."

Charles was used to being the person who described other people. He was not used to reading about himself!

Charles and Catherine returned to England on June 29, 1842. Another of Catherine's sisters, Georgina, came to live with them. Charles was happy to be away from America, a country he

AMERICAN NOTES

for

GENERAL CIRCULATION

By CHARLES DICKENS

LONDON
CHAPMAN AND HALL

described as "driven by a herd of rascals."

Chapter 5
Scrooges and Micawbers

In December 1843, Charles finished a story about a mean old man visited by three ghosts on Christmas Eve.

Jacob Marley warns of the three ghosts.

A Christmas Carol was published as a small book bound in red cloth with gold edging on its pages. It sold six thousand copies in just five days!

A Christmas Carol was a sensation.

In January, the Dickenses welcomed another son, Francis. Charles and Catherine now had five children.

Charles's daughter Mamie once said her father
wrote furiously at his desk, then jumped up and
went to the mirror. He made all sorts of faces,
then ran back to write more. Again and again
he returned to the mirror, acting out scenes and
talking out loud. He didn't even see Mamie there.
He had completely become the characters he was
hard at work creating.

Those characters had finally brought Charles the
security he longed for as a child. Now that Charles
had money, he wanted to use it to help others.

A CHRISTMAS CAROL

A *CHRISTMAS CAROL* NOT ONLY CHANGED THE
WAY PEOPLE THOUGHT ABOUT CHARLES DICKENS,
IT CHANGED THE WAY PEOPLE THOUGHT ABOUT
CHRISTMAS. SOME HISTORIANS BELIEVE THAT
MANY OF OUR HOLIDAY TRADITIONS, SUCH AS
PARTIES, FAMILY GATHERINGS, CHRISTMAS FEASTS,
DANCING, AND GAMES, WERE INSPIRED BY THE BOOK.

THE NAME "SCROOGE" CAME TO REFER TO
ANY STINGY, UNKIND PERSON, JUST AS "BAH,
HUMBUG!" CAME TO MEAN "THAT'S NONSENSE!"
EVEN THE PHRASE "MERRY CHRISTMAS!" WAS
MADE POPULAR BY THE BOOK. A FEW MONTHS
AFTER ITS PUBLICATION, THERE WAS A SURGE OF
MONEY GIVEN TO CHARITIES IN BRITAIN. PEOPLE
WERE INSPIRED TO BE GENEROUS! IN AMERICA,
A FACTORY OWNER WAS SO MOVED BY THE STORY
THAT HE GAVE ALL HIS WORKERS CHRISTMAS DAY
OFF AND GAVE EACH ONE OF THEM A TURKEY!

None of Charles's new friends knew about his family's past, except John Forster. John was the only person Charles ever told about it, but in 1849, Charles started work on *David Copperfield*. This book borrowed many details from real life— Charles's father's spending, the debtors' prison, leaving school for the factory, his mean landlady— and turned them into a best seller. So many people read *David Copperfield* that the book began to influence the way people spoke. A man who was always in debt but cheerfully expected that money would come from somewhere became known as a "Micawber" after a character in the book.

David Copperfield with his friend, Mr. Micawber

URANIA COTTAGE

IN MAY 1846, CHARLES, ALONG WITH AN
HEIRESS NAMED ANGELA BURDETT-COUTTS,
FOUNDED A HOME FOR HOMELESS WOMEN.

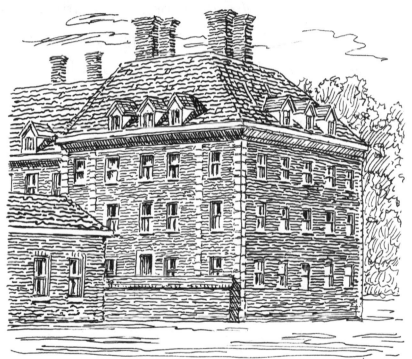

CHARLES DIDN'T WANT THE WOMEN BLAMED FOR
THEIR PROBLEMS. HE WANTED TO EDUCATE THEM
AND PROVIDE TRAINING FOR HOUSEHOLD SKILLS.
HE WANTED TO GIVE THEM HOPE.

MORE THAN ONE HUNDRED WOMEN GRADUATED
FROM URANIA COTTAGE BETWEEN 1847 AND 1859.

Charles's friends all recognized that "Micawber" was John Dickens, but they still never suspected that he had ever been in debtors' prison.

At the end of that year, Charles, who had left his job at *Bentley's Miscellany* some years earlier, decided to start his own monthly magazine called *Household Words*. It contained stories by Charles and his friends William Thackeray and Wilkie Collins.

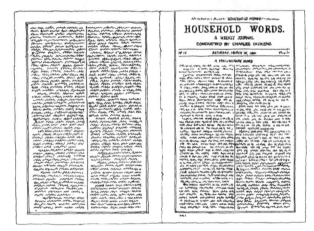

In August 1850, Catherine had her ninth child, Dora Annie Dickens. It wasn't easy for Catherine to be pregnant so often. Her sister

WILKIE COLLINS (1824–1889)

WILLIAM WILKIE COLLINS WAS A NOVELIST, PLAYWRIGHT, AND CLOSE FRIEND OF CHARLES DICKENS. HIS MOST FAMOUS NOVELS INCLUDE *THE WOMAN IN WHITE* AND *THE MOONSTONE*, THE FIRST DETECTIVE NOVEL IN THE ENGLISH LANGUAGE. *THE MOONSTONE* WAS HIS MOST POPULAR NOVEL AND PAVED THE WAY FOR OTHER FICTIONAL DETECTIVE STORIES SUCH AS THE SHERLOCK HOLMES MYSTERIES. HE SAID OF HIS EARLY DAYS WITH DICKENS, "WE SAW EACH OTHER EVERY DAY, AND WERE AS FOND OF EACH OTHER AS MEN COULD BE."

Georgina often took care of the children. Catherine didn't see Charles much because he was always working. She couldn't even take a walk with him because he walked too fast.

He said his inspiration came from the crowded streets. He sometimes walked for thirty miles at a time! The more tired Catherine became, the more energy Charles seemed to have.

In 1851, when Dora was still a baby, John Dickens died from complications of an operation on his gallbladder. No matter how much trouble his father had caused him, Charles forgave him and paid off every one of his debts.

Two weeks after his father's death, baby Dora suddenly died. Charles was heartbroken, but—as always—he kept working.

Chapter 6
Back to Gad's Hill

Between Charles's new
book, *Bleak House, Household
Words,* and Urania Cottage,
he had little time to relax.
When he had a kidney
infection, he took only six
days off work.

Catherine had had her
tenth and last child, Edward, in 1852.
In his letters to friends, Charles started to mention
trouble at home. He and Catherine were growing
apart, but Charles never said why. In Charles's
next novel, *Hard Times*, the hero was married to
a woman who wasn't right for him, but the law
wouldn't let him divorce her.

Many thought this was a reflection of the Dickenses' own marriage.

Charley Dickens, now eighteen, was at school at Eton. Charles planned to send his second son, Walter, to India to work for a British company. To others, Charles's family looked perfect— like the families in the stories he often wrote about in his magazine.

WALTER AND CHARLEY DICKENS

In February 1855, on a visit to Chatham,
Charles saw that the house he had liked so much
on Gad's Hill was for sale. Charles decided to buy
it. He had worked hard for many years, and now
he was going to live in the very house he had once
admired.

In November of that same year, Charles and
Wilkie Collins were writing a play together called
The Frozen Deep. It was based on the Franklin
expedition, a group of English explorers who had
gotten lost in the Arctic ten years earlier in 1845.

Their frozen bodies had recently been discovered.

The play was about the explorers' last days. Charles played the starring role of the expedition's leader, Richard Wardour. He was also the play's director and stage manager.

The Frozen Deep was a big success in England. People loved how Charles played the doomed Richard Wardour. Charles's daughters Mamie and Katey had parts in the show, as did his sister-in-law Georgina. They even gave a private performance for Queen Victoria.

In August 1857, not long after sixteen-year-old Walter Dickens left for India, Charles was invited to perform *The Frozen Deep* at the Free Trade Hall.

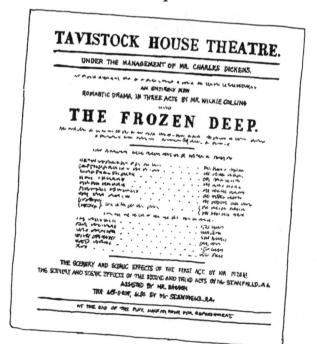

It was a big theater. Charles would need professional actresses to put the show on in that large a space. A friend recommended Frances Ternan and her three daughters, Fanny, Maria, and Ellen, who was known as Nelly.

QUEEN VICTORIA (1819–1901)

QUEEN VICTORIA WAS THE RULING MONARCH OF THE UNITED KINGDOM OF GREAT BRITAIN AND IRELAND FROM JUNE 1837 UNTIL HER DEATH IN 1901. SHE HELPED MAINTAIN PEACE AND PROSPERITY IN HER COUNTRY, AND SHE RULED DURING A TIME IN WHICH EXCITING NEW DISCOVERIES WERE MADE IN MANY FIELDS, INCLUDING SCIENCE, INDUSTRY, ENGINEERING, RECREATION, AND MEDICINE.

THE SPAN OF HER REIGN IS SO IMPORTANT THAT THE NINETEENTH CENTURY IN ENGLAND IS KNOWN AS THE VICTORIAN ERA. MANY GREAT ENGLISH NOVELS WERE WRITTEN AT THIS TIME, INCLUDING *ALICE'S ADVENTURES IN WONDERLAND* AND *JANE EYRE*, AS WELL AS THE *ADVENTURES OF SHERLOCK HOLMES* STORIES.

Chapter 7
The Worst of Times

Nelly Ternan was only eighteen years old when she met Charles. His friends knew that he loved her dearly, but publicly Charles said they were just friends. Catherine never spoke badly of Charles. She accepted his wish that they now live mostly apart.

NELLY TERNAN

By 1858, Charles lived at Gad's Hill with his children and their aunt Georgina. Catherine lived in London with a housekeeper. Laws at the time made divorce so expensive that hardly anyone could afford to do it. They agreed to lead separate lives instead.

Charles's life was busier than ever. When a friend of his died, Charles wanted to raise money for his family. He wrote a new version of *A Christmas Carol* to read for an audience. He played all the characters, using different voices.

The audience loved it. Charles, too, loved the performances—and the money they brought in. He went on a three-month tour in England, Scotland, and Ireland reading his work.

There was a lot of gossip about the Dickenses' marriage. This made Charles furious.

If Charles's friends stood up for Catherine, Charles no longer considered them friends! He even fought about it with the other workers at *Household Words*. In January 1859, he announced he was shutting down the magazine. He even stopped working on behalf of Urania Cottage.

Charles's friends were horrified at how he was acting and so were his children. He now claimed that they had never loved Catherine and she never loved them. When the children spoke to their mother, he got angry at them. His daughter Katey later said that her father "behaved like a madman."

The house on Gad's Hill had become a terrible, sad place. Katey escaped by marrying Wilkie Collins's sickly brother, Charles, an artist, in July 1860. On Katey's wedding day, Mamie found her father holding Katey's wedding dress and crying.

He blamed himself for driving her away from home. Catherine wasn't even invited to the wedding.

Charles put his energy into a new magazine, *All the Year Round*. Charles decided to publish his next novel as a serial in its pages. It was about the French Revolution. Charles had a rough time getting started on the story.

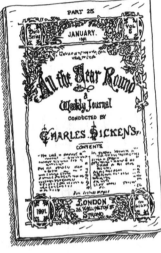

In time, the opening of *A Tale of Two Cities* became one of the most famous first lines of any book ever written: "It was the best of times, it was the worst of times."

Chapter 8
New Journeys

In the neighborhood of Gad's Hill there was a cemetery. One family had thirteen gravestones marking thirteen children who had died. It gave Charles an idea for a story called *Great Expectations*. It would be published in *All the Year Round* after *A Tale of Two Cities*. The story begins in a graveyard.

Young Pip

A poor young orphan, Pip, runs into an escaped convict there. Years later, Pip is given the chance to become a gentleman and join polite society.

After *Great Expectations,* Charles went on more reading tours. With so many broken relationships in his life, he took great comfort from audiences who loved him for his work. In September 1863, his mother died, but Charles didn't feel the kind of forgiveness for her that he'd felt for his father. He always remembered that it was his mother who wanted him to return to his job at Warren's.

Two months later, in December 1863, Charles's son Walter died in India.

In June 1865, Charles, Nelly, and Nelly's mother were on a train to London.

While crossing a bridge in Kent, the train jumped the tracks. It broke in two parts. Charles and the Ternans were thrown into one corner of a train car that hung halfway off the bridge. Charles later described the scene to a friend:

"No imagination can conceive the ruin of the carriages, or the extraordinary weights under which the people were lying, or the complications into which they were twisted up among iron and wood, and mud and water."

Charles climbed out through the window and got the Ternans to a waiting ambulance train.

He went back to help others trapped in the wreckage. He sat with the injured and the dying. Then he climbed back into his own carriage to retrieve the book he had been working on: *Our Mutual Friend.*

The following year, Charles planned a special tour to the United States.

Charles's second visit to America in 1867 was better than his first visit back in 1842. Crowds loved his readings. He saw old friends. Instead of facing questions about his book sales, he was performing for fans who welcomed him and cheered for his characters.

Charles's health was not the best. His foot was sometimes so swollen he couldn't walk, and he had trouble eating. Yet he traveled from Boston to New York to Philadelphia to Washington, DC. President Andrew Johnson even attended a reading and invited him to the White House.

Charles didn't regret returning to the United States one bit. On the boat home, in May 1868, he was already planning another reading tour.

KATE WIGGIN (1856—1923)

ON A TRAIN FROM MAINE TO BOSTON, A TWELVE-YEAR-OLD GIRL FROM PHILADELPHIA SLIPPED INTO THE SEAT BESIDE THE GREAT AUTHOR CHARLES DICKENS. SHE'D READ ALL HIS BOOKS SEVERAL TIMES, BUT "OF COURSE [SHE DID] SKIP SOME OF THE VERY DULL PARTS ONCE IN A WHILE; NOT THE SHORT DULL PARTS, BUT THE LONG ONES." THEY TALKED ABOUT WHICH PARTS WERE DULL AND WHICH BOOKS WERE THEIR FAVORITES—THEY BOTH LOVED *DAVID COPPERFIELD* BEST. KATE WIGGIN NEVER

FORGOT HER WONDERFUL TRIP WITH HER FAVORITE AUTHOR, EVEN AFTER SHE GREW UP TO BECOME A BEST-SELLING AUTHOR HERSELF. KATE WIGGIN PUBLISHED *REBECCA OF SUNNYBROOK FARM* IN 1903.

Chapter 9
Terror to the End

Some might have expected Charles Dickens to spend the summer of 1868 resting after his trip. Instead, he was planning a new, secret performance that would surprise all his friends.

At the end of the summer, his son Henry left for Trinity Hall at Cambridge University to study mathematics. Edward was going to join his brother Alfred farming in Australia.

Charles started his reading tour in October. In November, Charley became an editor at *All the Year Round*.

That same month, Charles unveiled the secret scene he was planning to perform. In *Oliver Twist,* a criminal named Bill Sykes catches his girlfriend, Nancy, trying to help the orphan, Oliver. In a fit of rage, he kills her. Terrified of what he's done, he runs away and is later killed by the police. Charles was going to perform it all onstage.

The scene was exciting and terrifying. Charles threw himself into the part of the evil Bill Sykes, whipping himself into a frenzy that was almost too real for his audience. In his own copy of the scene, Charles made a note to himself: "Terror to the End." That's exactly what he gave audiences.

When it was finished, he was so exhausted he had to be helped offstage. But once he felt better, he wanted to do it again. Like any great actor, he loved the power he had over the audience.

His doctor ordered him to quit the tour completely, but Charles refused. The doctor told Charley Dickens to go to every performance.

If his father seemed like he was going to fall down, the doctor had told him, "You must run up there and catch him . . . or, by Heaven, he'll die before them all!" In April 1869, Charles took a break from the tour, but he wouldn't quit completely.

While resting, Charles signed a contract with Chapman and Hall for a new book to be written in twelve parts: *The Mystery of Edwin Drood*.

For the illustrations in this new book, Charles hoped to hire his son-in-law, Charles Collins. Katey's husband needed the money, but he was too sick to do the work. Charles had never liked Katey marrying someone so unwell. He later said that Charles Collins had just "collapsed for the whole term of his natural life." For someone as active as Charles Dickens,

Charles Collins must have been difficult to understand.

Charles's foot was still painful, and one of his arms was numb. He had probably had a stroke, but ignored it. He couldn't come downstairs at Gad's Hill for most of Christmas 1869. One evening, he joined some of his family for traditional parlor games. In a memory game,

everyone had to recite a list of items and add one more item for the next person. When they had been playing for a while, his son Henry said, Charles "had successfully gone through the long string of words, and finished up with his own contribution: 'Warren's Blacking, 30 Strand!'"

THE DICKENS CHILDREN

ALL OF CATHERINE AND CHARLES'S CHILDREN WERE GIVEN SPECIAL NICKNAMES BY THEIR FATHER. ALL LIVED VERY DIFFERENT LIVES:

CHARLES—CHARLEY—BECAME AN EDITOR AT *ALL AROUND THE WORLD.*

MAMIE—MILD GLO'STER—NEVER MARRIED, LIVED WITH HER AUNT GEORGINA AFTER CHARLES'S DEATH.

KATEY—LUCIFER BOX—BECAME A WIDOW AND THEN MARRIED AN ARTIST AND BECAME AN ARTIST HERSELF.

WALTER—YOUNG SKULL—DIED YOUNG IN INDIA.

FRANCIS—CHICKENSTALKER—JOINED THE MOUNTED POLICE IN CANADA.

ALFRED—SAMPSON BRASS OR SKITTLES— BECAME A FARMER IN AUSTRALIA.

SYDNEY—THE OCEAN SPECTRE OR THE ADMIRAL— BECAME AN OFFICER IN THE ROYAL NAVY.

HENRY—MR. H—BECAME A VERY RESPECTED JUDGE.

EDWARD—THE PLORNISHGHENTER OR PLORN— WENT INTO POLITICS IN AUSTRALIA.

Charles said it with a strange look in his eye, as if the words had special meaning for him. Henry didn't know what that meaning could be. Nearly fifty years later, Charles was still haunted by the shame of having worked in the blacking factory and still kept it a secret from almost everyone.

Chapter 10
Poet's Corner

Charles Dickens was no longer the boy in the window at Warren's blacking factory. He was the most popular writer in the world. He'd written over fifteen novels. He'd traveled all over Europe and North America. He'd been chased by adoring crowds. He'd appeared in front of theaters packed with fans. His books were translated into many languages. Even his least popular books sold well. He received letters from all over the world. He'd created words that had been added to the dictionary. Where once his family had been threatened with eviction from their home, he now owned more than one beautiful house, including the one he'd dreamed of living in as a child. Amazingly, he'd stayed popular for decades.

The first chapter of *Edwin Drood* appeared on March 31, 1870. It sold an amazing fifty thousand copies in its first few days of release. Thirty-four years after the publication of *The Pickwick Papers*, Charles Dickens was a sensation all over again. "As he delighted the fathers, so he delights the children," said the London *Times*.

Every morning at Gad's Hill, Charles wrote in

a small Swiss chalet given to him by a friend who sent it in pieces from Switzerland. Charles loved writing in the upper story where the mirrors on the walls reflected the trees and the river outside.

On June 4, 1870, Katey came for a visit. They had a long talk. Katey was surprised by the kind of things her father said. He told her he wished he'd been a better father and a better man.

He talked about his relationship with Nelly and the end of his marriage. He spoke, Katey later said, "as though his life was over and there was nothing left."

Katey left the next day. On June 8, Charles spent the morning in the chalet, writing. It was unusual for Charles to work in the afternoon, but on this day, after lunch, he returned to finish chapter six of *Edwin Drood*.

That evening at dinner with his sister-in-law Georgina, Charles had a stroke. Katey and Mamie rushed home to see him. He died the following day without ever waking up. It was June 9, 1870. Charles Dickens was only fifty-eight years old.

Charles had planned to be buried near Rochester Cathedral, but his country would accept nothing less than Westminster Abbey. Westminster Abbey is the most famous church in England. Many of the greatest writers in English history are buried there in what is called Poet's Corner. When Charles died, the London *Times* wrote an editorial saying he should be buried in Poet's Corner. The Dean of Westminster agreed and offered to bury him there. It was a great honor—one Charles's family could not refuse.

CHARLES DICKENS
BORN 7TH FEBRUARY 1812
DIED 9TH JUNE 1870

Charles had earned his place among the greatest British writers. He was buried in a small, private ceremony, but so many people came to bring flowers that the church had to keep the grave open for two days to hold all the crowds.

People from all walks of life made their way to
Westminster Abbey to say good-bye to him.

There was no other person in England so beloved by people of all classes, rich and poor. To this day, a wreath is laid on his grave every year on his birthday.

The very next year, John Forster published a biography of his friend Charles Dickens.

For the first time, people learned that Charles did not have the happy childhood that his readers assumed he had. They learned just how much David Copperfield *was* Charles Dickens. They saw that Charles had sympathy for people in all parts of society because he had been both poor and rich. The part of his life that he had always hidden—the poverty, hard work, and shame of prison—was the very thing that made his writing so special and so loved by so many.

TIMELINE OF
CHARLES DICKENS'S LIFE

1812	—Charles Dickens born in Portsmouth
1817	—Dickens family moves to Chatham, England
1822	—Dickens family moves to London, England
1824	—Charles starts work in the blacking factory
1825	—Charles returns to school
1833	—"A Dinner at Poplar Walk" published in *Monthly Magazine*
1836	—Charles marries Catherine Hogarth
1837	—Catherine's sister Mary Hogarth dies
1842	—Charles visits the United States
1843	—*A Christmas Carol* is published
1846	—Urania Cottage is founded
1850	—First issue of *Household Words* is published
1854	—*Hard Times* is published
1857	—Charles separates from his wife
1859	—*A Tale of Two Cities* is published
1865	—Charles is in a train crash in Kent
1867	—Second tour of the United States
1870	—Charles Dickens dies

TIMELINE OF THE WORLD

Work on Westminster Abbey begins	EARLY 970s
Gutenberg printing press is invented in Germany	1450
Macbeth is written by William Shakespeare	c. 1606
Great Fire of London destroys much of the city	1666
Tom Jones by Henry Fielding is published	1749
Ludwig van Beethoven is born	1770
French Revolution begins	1787
Napoleon Bonaparte invades the Netherlands	1795
War of 1812 breaks out	1812
Japan closes its ports to foreign ships	1825
Poland revolts against Russian rule	1830
Victoria is crowned queen of England	1837
Devil's Island penal colony is opened	1852
Hollywood is founded	1857
First commercially sold typewriter is invented	1865

BIBLIOGRAPHY

* Manning, Mick, and Brita Granström. **Charles Dickens: Scenes from an Extraordinary Life**. London: Frances Lincoln Children's Books, 2011.

Slater, Michael. **Charles Dickens**. New Haven, CT: Yale University Press, 2009.

Smiley, Jane. **Charles Dickens: A Life**. New York: Penguin, 2002.

* Stanley, Diane, and Peter Vennema. **Charles Dickens: The Man Who Had Great Expectations**. New York: Morrow Junior Books, 1993.

Tomalin, Claire. **Charles Dickens: A Life**. New York: Penguin, 2011.

* Warren, Andrea. **Charles Dickens and the Street Children of London**. New York: Houghton Mifflin Books for Children, 2011.

* Books for young readers